21st Century Junior Library

Plateosaurus

by Josh Gregory

CHERRY LAKE PUBLISHING * ANN ARBOR, MICHIGAN

CHERRY
LAKE
Publishing

Published in the United States of America by Cherry Lake Publishing
Ann Arbor, Michigan
www.cherrylakepublishing.com

Content Adviser: Gregory M. Erickson, PhD, Paleontologist, Department of Biological Science, Florida State University, Tallahassee, Florida

Reading Adviser: Marla Conn, Read With Me Now

Photo Credits: Cover and pages 8, 10, 16, and 18, © Michael Rosskothen/Shutterstock.com; page 4, © The Natural History Museum/Alamy; page 6, Eva K. / tinyurl.com/kkbjx7d / CC-BY-SA-2.5; page 12, © leonello calvetti/Shutterstock.com; page 14, © Stocktrek Images, Inc./Alamy; page 20, Funk Monk / tinyurl.com/kctcndd / CC-BY-SA-3.0.

LIBRARY OF CONGRESS CATALOGING-IN-PUBLICATION DATA
Gregory, Josh, author.
  Plateosaurus / by Josh Gregory.
      pages cm.—(Dinosaurs) (21st century junior library)
  Summary: "Learn all about the dinosaur known as Plateosaurus, from where it lived to what it ate."—Provided by publisher.
  Audience: K to grade 3
  Includes bibliographical references and index.
  ISBN 978-1-63362-384-2 (lib. bdg.)—ISBN 978-1-63362-412-2 (pbk.)—
ISBN 978-1-63362-440-5 (pdf)—ISBN 978-1-63362-468-9 (e-book)
  1. Plateosaurus—Juvenile literature. 2. Dinosaurs—Juvenile literature. I. Title.
QE862.S3G7675 2016
567.913—dc23   2014045657

Cherry Lake Publishing would like to acknowledge the work of
The Partnership for 21st Century Skills.
Please visit www.p21.org for more information.

Printed in the United States of America
Corporate Graphics
July 2015

CONTENTS

Plateosaurus was larger than many other dinosaurs of its era.

What Was Plateosaurus?

Hundreds of millions of years ago, dinosaurs lived on Earth. Among them was *Plateosaurus*. It was one of the biggest dinosaurs of its time. But it was not a fearsome hunter. Instead, it was a peaceful plant eater.

This *Plateosaurus* skull can be seen at a museum in Germany.

Like all dinosaurs, *Plateosaurus* is now **extinct**. However, it was once common in what is now Europe. *Plateosaurus* lived between 214 million and 204 million years ago. We know about it from studying its **fossils**.

Look!

You can get a look at *Plateosaurus* fossils for yourself. Many museums have dinosaur fossils. Some even have entire *Plateosaurus* **skeletons**!

Plateosaurus had a long neck and tail.

What Did *Plateosaurus* Look Like?

The name *Plateosaurus* means "broad lizard." This is because the dinosaur was very wide at the shoulders. *Plateosaurus* was also very long. The largest ones found were about 33 feet (10 meters) long. However, they were only around 10 feet (3 m) tall.

Experts think *Plateosaurus* walked on two legs.

Plateosaurus had a thick, heavy body. It weighed almost 4,000 pounds (1,814 kilograms). That is heavier than a car! The dinosaur had strong back legs to carry this weight. Its front legs were smaller but still powerful.

Experts have learned a lot about *Plateosaurus's* size and shape from its skeleton.

Plateosaurus had a long tail and neck. Its head was very small compared to the rest of its body. It had a long, flat shape. The dinosaur's mouth was curved.

Create!

Scientists aren't sure what color *Plateosaurus*'s skin was. Draw your own picture of this dinosaur. Color it in. Be creative with the colors you use!

Plateosaurus bites off a piece from
an evergreen plant.

How Did
Plateosaurus Live?

Plateosaurus was an **herbivore**. This means it only ate plants. The dinosaur's body was perfectly built to eat a lot of leaves. Its long neck allowed it to reach high up into the trees. It could also feed on plants on the ground.

Plateosaurus teeth were made for snipping off and shredding plants.

Plateosaurus's teeth had jagged edges. This helped the dinosaur tear leaves off trees. *Plateosaurus* also had thumbs on its front feet. Each thumb ended in a long claw. These helped the dinosaur gather leaves and branches. They might also have helped it dig up tasty roots.

Members of a *Plateosaurus* herd looked out for one another.

Plateosaurus lived in groups called **herds**. A single herd could include hundreds of these dinosaurs. Herd members helped one another watch out for danger. They also likely traveled together in search of plants and water.

Make a Guess!

How do scientists know *Plateosaurus* lived in herds? Remember that we learn about dinosaurs by studying fossils. How could fossils show that a dinosaur lived in groups?

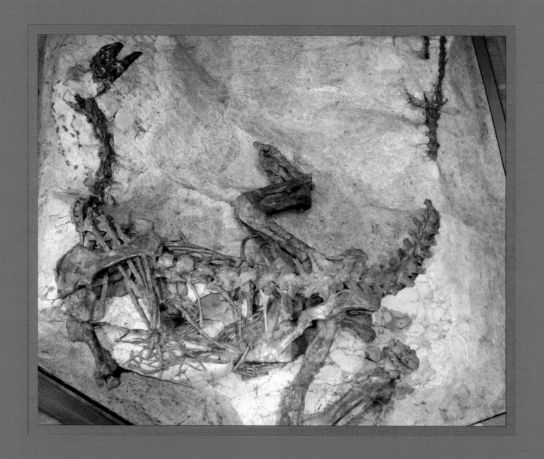

This *Plateosaurus* was found in Switzerland.